WHAT MAKES YOU
HAPPY

ANDY STANLEY

ZONDERVAN® NORTH POINT RESOURCES

ZONDERVAN

What Makes You Happy Participant's Guide
Copyright © 2017 by North Point Ministries, Inc.

This title is also available as a Zondervan ebook.

Requests for information should be addressed to:
Zondervan, *3900 Sparks Dr. SE, Grand Rapids, Michigan 49546*

ISBN 978-0-310-08499-0

First Printing November 2016 / Printed in the United States of America

[CONTENTS]

USING THE PARTICIPANT'S GUIDE

[BEFORE SESSION ONE]

1. Read through pages 7–9 to gain an overview of the study.

2. Read through A Typical Group Meeting on page 80 to gain an understanding of the flow of this study.

3. Read through the content in Session One on pages 11–16.

[DURING EACH GROUP MEETING]

1. Turn to the Video Notes page, and watch the video segment.

2. Use the Discussion Questions to have a conversation about the video content.

3. Read the Think About It section aloud.

4. Review the Before the Next Session homework at the end of the chapter.

[INTRODUCTION]

We all want to be happy. But let's face it: great art and literature throughout history have been based on the premise that an awful lot of people—maybe even most people—go through life with a deep sense of yearning. There's something inside them that feels empty. No matter how much they achieve or acquire, that emptiness doesn't go away. It's as if they can catch a glimpse of happiness, but they can't quite ever get hold of it. And once they've chased after the false promise of happiness for long enough, they begin to suspect that happiness doesn't even exist. They lose hope. They give up.

Here's the good news: it *is* possible to be happy. It *is* possible to fill that empty space inside.

The title of this study could be a question—"What makes you happy?"—but it could also be a statement. It might even be a promise. Over the next six sessions, we're going to tell you what makes you happy. The reason we'll tell you what makes you happy is that you may not know. The idea that you don't know what makes you happy may be surprising. It may even be offensive. After all, no one knows you better than you, right?

There's one way to tell if you know what makes you happy. If you keep chasing after happiness, but you're not happy, there's a good chance it's because you don't know what makes you happy. Imagine that.

If you think it's strange for someone who doesn't know you to promise to tell you what makes you happy, just remember that every time you open a magazine, listen to the radio, go on the Internet, or watch television, people you've never met in places you've never visited create shows, movies, books, and ads that tell you what will make you happy. Every single one of us has fallen for someone's promise of the secret of happiness at least once or twice . . . if not 100 times.

As we'll discover over the course of this study, it's impossible to market and sell true happiness. Quick-fix happiness can be marketed and sold, but not the real stuff—not lasting happiness. The path to true happiness is simple to understand but challenging to follow. It requires living with intentionality. It demands letting go of some of our most deeply held cultural assumptions. It means looking at the world around us through an entirely new set of lenses.

Few people in our culture are talking about what really makes us happy. So for the next few weeks, we're going to do just that. We're going to tell you what makes you happy.

SESSION ONE

[NOTHING]

If only I had . . . if only I drove . . . if only I wore . . . if only I knew . . . if only I won . . . then I would feel better about myself. Then I would be happy.

You've had thoughts like that, right? We all have. You spend a lot of time and money chasing after happiness, but it always feels just out of reach. No matter what you do, no matter what you achieve, no matter how much you acquire, you're still not happy.

Here's what you need to understand: happiness is more about *who* than *what*. We learn this lesson early in life, but we tend to forget it as we grow older. We learned it in the backyard when we were playing with a bunch of *"whos."* It didn't matter what we had. It didn't matter what we didn't have. It mattered who we were with. When we were in elementary school, middle school, and high school, it didn't matter what we had as long as we were with the right bunch of *"whos."* Isn't that true?

Happiness is always associated with a who or two.

If happiness were about a what, we could just go out and get our happy "what"s and we'd be happy all the time. It wouldn't matter how people treated us.

The problem is that happy "what" always leads to happy "what else." That's because happy "what" is like caffeine. It wears off over time. You were as excited about your old phone when you first bought it as you are about your new phone. Soon, your new phone won't be new anymore and you won't be excited about it. You'll need a new one. Same with your car. Same with your job.

If an aging "what" deflates your happiness, you weren't happy to begin with. You were just on the receiving end of good marketing.

Happiness is about "who." At the end of their lives, people don't have possessional regrets. They have relational regrets. They don't long for more stuff. They long for better, healthier connections with others.

Happy people are at peace. They have peace with themselves,

others, and God. Any thing or behavior that undermines peace in any of those relationships undermines their happiness.

WHO, NOT WHAT

Every so often you'll hear someone say, "I don't need anyone to be happy." But people who say that fall into one of two categories. Either they have so many relational options, they don't know what it's like to be isolated, or they don't know how to fix their isolation so they tell themselves they're fine. Again, relationally disconnected people aren't happy. God made us for other people. And connection to God is the foundation of happiness.

One thing Jesus followers have discovered *is that peace with God paves the way to peace with ourselves and equips us to make peace with others.* When you begin to view yourself in a right relationship with your Creator, something happens on the inside. That peace with God frees us to find peace with ourselves and equips us to make peace with others. In fact, most of the New Testament is about how to be at peace with other people.

Jesus was asked a lot of silly questions in the New Testament because the religious leaders of his day were always trying to trick him into saying something offensive or controversial that would turn the crowd against him. One time a legal expert asked him what he thought God's favorite law was. Jesus' answer influences how his followers understand and prioritize relationships.

Jewish people in first-century Palestine lived by over 600 religious laws. Keeping the law was a significant part of their daily lives. There was a generally accepted answer to the question of which law was most important to God, but the lawyer wanted Jesus to weigh in. Here's what happened:

One of them, an expert in the law, tested him with this question: "Teacher, which is the greatest commandment in the Law?"

Jesus replied: "'Love the Lord your God with all your heart and with all your soul and with all your mind.' This is the first and greatest commandment. And the second is like it: 'Love your neighbor as yourself.' All the Law and the Prophets hang on these two commandments."

Matthew 22: 35–40

Jesus' answer is simple, direct, and relational. What's the most important law? Love God. What's almost as important as loving God? Loving other people. In fact, those two laws are so significant, Jesus said that if you obeyed them, you wouldn't have to pay attention to the other 598 laws. You'd already be keeping all of God's laws if you did those two things.

Jesus' answer is profound because he said that the most important things in life are peace with God, peace with others, and peace with ourselves. That's the definition of happiness, which means that Jesus wants us to be happy. God created us with the capacity for happiness, and then told us in no uncertain terms how to be happy. This pursuit of happiness—of peace—isn't a secondary concern. It's core to who we are.

We tend to assume that God gets in the way of our happiness. We believe we can either be good religious people, or we can be happy. We can't be both. We won't stay in unhappy circumstances for long, so we leave church. We drift away from our heavenly Father. That's tragic. The truth is, when we resist God, we resist happiness. God provides the way to happiness. If you talk to people about their greatest regrets, you'll find more often than not that those regrets were the results of unhealthy pursuits of happiness in isolation from God. We create regrets when we abandon peace with ourselves, others, and God.

That separation is called "sin." When you experience relational conflict, it's because somebody sinned. Sin also separates us from God. That's because when you sin against another person, you sin against someone God loves. You can't be okay *with* God and wrong with someone God loves. You can't mistreat his children and expect to be on good relational terms with him. John 3:16 says, "For God so loved the world that he gave his only Son." So, when you mistreat another person, you are out of sorts with God, not just that other person.

Watch the video segment for Session One, using the space provided below to take notes on anything that stands out to you.

VIDEO NOTES

DISCUSSION QUESTIONS

1. What's the first thing that comes to mind when you think about what makes you happy? Why do you think that comes to mind?

2. How would you define the word "happiness?" How do you think your definition has influenced the ways you've chosen to pursue happiness?

3. Read Matthew 22:35–40 on page 14. Respond to Jesus' statement. Does it sound too easy? Why or why not?

4. During the message, Andy said that sin separates us from ourselves, others, and God by enticing us to substitute things for relationships. Do you believe this to be true? Why or why not?

5. Are you at peace with yourself, others, and God? If not, what's getting in the way of your peace in those relationships?

6. In *what* are you currently seeking happiness? What is one thing you can do this week to turn your attention to Jesus as your source of happiness? What can this group do to support you?

THINK ABOUT IT

Happiness is about "who," not "what." Happy people are at peace with God, others, and themselves. Sin undermines peace because it separates you from God, others, and yourself by substituting things for people. Sin makes a happy promise it can't keep. Sin isn't your friend. Sin kills relationships.

James, the brother of Jesus, wrote: Then, after desire has conceived, it gives birth to sin; and sin, when it is full-grown, gives birth to death (James 1:15).

When we opt for sin, we undermine our happiness and the happiness of those closest to us. This stands in stark contrast to what we are all tempted to believe: that God keeps us from happiness. But ask yourself these questions:

- Has sin made my life better or worse?
- Has sin contributed to my relationships or undermined them?

BEFORE THE NEXT SESSION

Read pages 23–29 for an overview of next session's content.

[**PLAN FOR IT**]

Jesus' Sermon on the Mount includes what are traditionally called the "Beatitudes." They're a series of observations about how to live that all begin with the word "blessed."

"Blessed are the poor in spirit,

for theirs is the kingdom of heaven.

Blessed are those who mourn,

for they will be comforted.

Blessed are the meek,

for they will inherit the earth.

Blessed are those who hunger and thirst for righteousness,

for they will be filled.

Blessed are the merciful,

for they will be shown mercy.

Blessed are the pure in heart,

for they will see God.

Blessed are the peacemakers,

for they will be called children of God.

Blessed are those who are persecuted because of

righteousness, for theirs is the kingdom of heaven.

Blessed are you when people insult you, persecute you
and falsely say all kinds of evil against you because of
me. Rejoice and be glad, because great is your reward in
heaven, for in the same way they persecuted the prophets
who were before you." Matthew 5:3–12

The Beatitudes are a series of statements in which Jesus explodes
nearly every myth about happiness. Do you think you'd be happy
if you were wealthy? Jesus says being rich or poor doesn't make a

person happy. People who are poor in spirit are happy. That sounds strange, but what Jesus means is that people who depend on God in all aspects of their lives are happy.

Do you think you'd be happy if life was never difficult? Jesus says those who mourn are happy. That's an especially strange claim. What he means is that people who are emotionally connected don't hide or run from bad things in the world. They face moments of sorrow, grief, and death head-on. They embrace the fact that death is a part of life. We tend to sanitize death in order to reduce our fear of it. But that's just suppressing the fear, not overcoming it. And people who fear death can't be happy.

Do you think happiness is being the captain of your own destiny? Jesus says the meek are happy. Meekness has a negative connotation in our culture, because we associate it with weakness. But when Jesus talks about the meek, he means people who have accurate estimations of themselves within the context of God's creation and love. Meek people understand that God is up to something in the world and that they're invited to participate, even though it's not all about them.

When Jesus says, "Blessed are those who hunger and thirst for righteousness," he's talking about people who live without guilt or regret. Making a commitment to do the right thing even when it costs us something leads to happiness. That's definitely not a message we receive from our culture. But just imagine how much peace you'd have if you could live with a perfectly clear conscience.

NO REGRET

Isn't it true that the regrets we wish we could erase from our lives are related to bad decisions? When Jesus says that those who hunger and thirst for righteousness will be filled, that's not a popular sentiment. It may not even make sense to us. But it gets to the heart of one of the keys of happiness: living without regret.

Jesus follows up his statement about those who hunger and thirst for righteousness by saying, "Blessed are the merciful, for they will be shown mercy." What he means is that people who are relationally generous are happy. Merciful people don't hold grudges. They don't seek revenge. They forgive. They don't succumb to bitterness. They don't wait for people who wronged them in the past to make things right.

That may not seem fair, but it's still true. When we withhold mercy and forgiveness—even from people who don't deserve it—it harms us. You've never met a happy bitter person. You've never met a happy person who holds grudges. You've never met a happy person who's waiting for payback.

But you've probably met people who were extraordinarily mistreated but emerged from those unfair circumstances happy. When you dig beneath the surface of their stories, you discover they are men and women who understand what it means to be relationally generous. They decided to extend mercy and forgiveness to people who didn't deserve either. When Jesus says that people who extend mercy will receive mercy, he's not talking about karma. He means that radical relational generosity leads to happiness. Being merciful to those who wrong you is being merciful to you, because you're setting yourself up for peace.

Jesus builds on this idea of relational generosity when he says, "Blessed are the pure in heart, for they will see God." Would you like to see life so clearly that you recognize where God is at work? Would you like to be able to recognize God's plan for your life?

Would you like to recognize what God wants you to do in difficult situations regarding your relationships, your money, your career, or your future? Would you like to be able to look at opportunities and see which lead to trouble and which lead to a regret-free life?

Who would say no to those questions?

According to Jesus, that kind of clarity is found in moral and ethical purity. Purifying your mind means deciding that you don't have to experience everything in life to understand life. Steering clear of sin provides the greatest opportunity to see God's activity in the world. We waste time and energy worrying that we'll miss out if we follow Jesus. He says we'll miss out if we don't follow him. We'll miss what God wants to do in us and through us. And that offers true happiness. Sin offers a false promise of happiness.

"Blessed are the peacemakers, for they will be called children of God." Do you know any happy troublemakers? Of course not. Troublemakers are troubled by other people's happiness. Troublemakers target happy people because troublemakers want everyone to be unhappy. Reconcilers are happy. People who are willing to walk into broken relationships and make peace are happy.

Finally, Jesus says, "Blessed are those who are persecuted because of righteousness, for theirs is the kingdom of heaven." That sounds like a huge cost for happiness, right? None of us wants to be persecuted. None of us wants to suffer. We don't want to lose our jobs for doing the right thing. We don't want to fail tests because we're the only ones who didn't cheat. We don't want to lose the deal because we weren't willing to lie like the other person. When we experience persecution in whatever form it takes, we don't feel blessed.

But here's what Jesus meant. We will all suffer in this life. There's no avoiding it. We can be happy if we suffer for doing the right thing. We can be at peace. But when we suffer for doing the wrong thing, we're left with guilt and regret. We have no peace with God, ourselves, or other people.

Happiness is a result. Happiness is about wisdom now that leads to peace later. Happiness is not immediately accessible. You can't hear a song or read a book and be instantly happy. Happiness is like the work of a farmer. It follows the law of the harvest. You sow and reap your way to happiness.

Watch the video segment for Session Two, using the space provided below to take notes on anything that stands out to you.

VIDEO NOTES

DISCUSSION QUESTIONS

1. Last week, you were challenged to turn your attention to Jesus as your source for happiness. How did it go?

2. How would you define the word "holiness"? How do you think your definition has influenced your relationship with God?

3. Read Matthew 5:3–12 on pages 23–24. Do you have trouble believing that happiness follows from the list of behaviors Jesus describes? Why or why not?

4. What are some reasons it's difficult for us to live as though we're dependent on God? What do we lose when we live like that? What do we gain?

5. Read Matthew 7:24–26 below. To what extent have you built your life upon dependence on God? How do you think that has affected your happiness?

    > Therefore everyone who hears these words of mine and puts them into practice is like a wise man who built his house on the rock. The rain came down, the streams rose, and the winds blew and beat against that house; yet it did not fall, because it had its foundation on the rock. But everyone who hears these words of mine and does not put them into practice is like a foolish man who built his house on sand. Matthew 7:24–26

6. If happiness is powered by the law of the harvest, what do you need to "sow" in your life right now so that you can "reap" happiness in the future? How can this group support you?

THINK ABOUT IT

Life is difficult for all of us. We face obstacles, suffer setbacks, and miss opportunities. It's easy to allow those things to rob us of happiness. It's tempting to assume that happiness is a result of our circumstances. If we can control our circumstances, then we will be happy. That's a lie that always leads to disappointment and frustration.

Wise people don't find happiness in their circumstances. Wise people recognize their dependence on God and find happiness in that dependence.

God has set things up so that happiness is subject to the law of the harvest. It's an outcome. It's a result. You sow and reap your way into happiness.

BEFORE THE NEXT SESSION

Read pages 35–41 for an overview of next session's content.

[PEACE WITH GOD]

Happy people are at peace with other people.

Happy people aren't angry.

Happy people aren't bitter.

Happy people don't seek revenge.

Happy people don't see themselves as victims.

Happy people are at peace with the world around them.

Truly happy people are at peace with God.

Peace with God is important, because one of the things the New Testament says is that it paves the way to peace with ourselves and equips us to make peace with others. If you aren't at peace with yourself, it's because of something in your past that you regret or feel guilty about. You can't seem to get away from it.

When you make peace with God, he paves the way forward so you can find peace with yourself. But the big idea in the New Testament is that peace with God equips us to make peace with other people. The central ethic in the New Testament is this: do unto others as your heavenly Father through Jesus has done unto you. Christians are required to forgive because we've been forgiven. When we make peace with God through Christ, we understand our obligation to figure out how to treat people the way our heavenly Father treated us. That's how peace with God equips us to make peace with other people.

When we talk about making peace with God, it assumes there's conflict with God. The New Testament teaches that there is conflict between God and us. The source of that conflict is sin—both sin in general and our personal sin. We were all born into sin, just like we were born in a particular nation. We are sinners the same way we are Americans or Koreans or Nigerians. We didn't have a choice in the matter. How did we get here? The New Testament and Jewish Old Testament teach that sin entered the world through human beings. God didn't create sin. God created people, and people created sin. It's so hardwired into us that having been born into sin, we commit personal sins.

And then there's personal sin—sin that's born of our behavior. The best way to understand our conflict with God is to think about the family you grew up in. As a child, at some point along the way, you were not at peace with your parents. That's what sin does to your relationship with God.

Wherever there is sin, there is death. Our sin kills relationships. It kills careers. Sometimes it kills our health. The New Testament explains something that we all experience every day. Wherever sin shows up in our lives, something dies. For some, it's why they can't get along with themselves. Sin kills self-esteem. Sin kills discipline.

Sin kills our relationships with others. It creates anger, bitterness, and hurt. It alienates us from those we should love—either because they've wronged us or we've wronged them.

We can't overcome sin by fixing our relationships with others or learning to love ourselves. That's backwards. For us to be at peace with ourselves and others, sin must be conquered. That requires the intervention of God.

REBIRTH

The first step to finding peace with God is to be reborn into a new nation. We have to leave the kingdom of sin and be accepted into the kingdom of God's beloved Son. Peace with God doesn't begin by trying to make you better. Peace with God doesn't begin with breaking bad habits. Peace with God doesn't begin with church attendance. Acting righteous doesn't make you righteous.

Peace with God begins with faith in Christ.

Your heavenly Father has accepted you into his nation, his kingdom. He has accepted you into his family. You get there by placing your faith, or your confidence, in what God has done for us through Jesus, his Son. Peace with God begins with faith in Christ.

The apostle Paul described the relationship between faith in Christ and peace with God like this:

Therefore, since we have been justified through faith, we have peace with God through our Lord Jesus Christ, through whom we have gained access by faith into this grace in which we now stand. And we boast in the hope of the glory of God. Romans 5:1–2

Faith in Christ means that we believe Jesus' death and resurrection repaired our relationship with God, which had been broken by sin.

Every parent knows something of the tension God experiences around sin. A parent's love is too strong to simply go along with self-destructive behavior in a child. God's love for you is too strong to go along with your sin. Just like a great parent, God will sometimes ding your conscience. He surfaces the tension between your happiness and your disobedience. He does this because he's a good Father. In Matthew 5:48, Jesus compares God to a perfect father. We all know God isn't a man. God is so different from us that Jesus knew the only way we could begin to understand him is if we thought of ourselves as relating to him the way a young child relates to a father. Like a great parent, God will not turn his back on you.

God doesn't hang onto bitterness. He doesn't hold grudges. He doesn't seek revenge. Instead, even before you were born, he sent his Son to die for your sins. He allowed you to receive his Son as your Savior, knowing you would continue to sin. He didn't kick you out of his family because good fathers never disinherit their kids. That's how Jesus says we are to view God.

The apostle John spent a lot of time face-to-face with Jesus. Decades later, in his old age, he wrote about what Jesus taught. He addressed what it means for a Christian to be out of sync with his or her heavenly Father. Here's what he wrote:

> If we claim to have fellowship with him and yet walk in the darkness, we lie and do not live out the truth. 1 John 1:6

If you pretend that you and God are on good terms, but you know you're living in disobedience to God, you lie to yourself and to the people around you. God wants you to have peace with him, but that won't happen if you ignore what he says.

Here's the thing: our relationships with others can affect our relationship with God. John explains it like this:

Whoever claims to love God yet hates a brother or sister is a liar. For whoever does not love their brother and sister, whom they have seen, cannot love God, whom they have not seen. 1 John 4:20

Why is that? Because God loves all people. As we said before, God isn't at peace with anyone who isn't at peace with those he loves. So here's a question: Are you at peace with God?

Until you can say yes to that question, you won't make peace with yourself or with other people. You won't be happy.

Watch the video segment for Session Three, using the space provided below to take notes on anything that stands out to you.

VIDEO NOTES

DISCUSSION QUESTIONS

1. Do you agree that peace with God paves the way to peace with ourselves and equips us to make peace with others? Why or why not?

2. To what extent do you think the word "sin" is relevant to your relationship with God?

3. Read Romans 5:1–2 on page 39. Does peace with God through Jesus Christ sound too easy? Why or why not?

4. Read 1 John 4:20 on page 41. What does this verse say about how God values you and other people? In what ways does it challenge your assumptions about what it means to have a relationship with God?

5. Talk about a time when you were in conflict with someone. How did that conflict affect your relationship with God?

6. What stands in the way of your peace with God? What's one thing you can do this week to begin to surrender that area of your life? What can this group do to support you?

THINK ABOUT IT

Sin separates. Don't let it continue to separate you from the One who loves you and knows what's best for you.

Peace with God is possible because God has made peace with you. Your heavenly Father is looking for you whether or not you are looking for him. Why refuse God's offer of peace? You can experience that peace when you stop resisting and striving and begin to surrender. Peace with God begins with faith in Christ. Peace with God is sustained by submission to Christ.

BEFORE THE NEXT SESSION

Read pages 47–51 for an overview of next session's content.

SESSION FOUR

[HAPPY MONEY]

How much money would it take to make you happy?

How much more *money would it take to give you peace? How much more money would it take to relieve the pressure, to give you some breathing room?*

We all know intuitively that there's a connection between money and happiness. The problem is, we're tempted to think that the degree of our happiness correlates with the amount of money we have. The truth is, the relationship between our happiness and our money is all about management.

If you mismanage your money, you undermine your peace. You know that's true. It doesn't matter how much money you have or how much money you earn. If you don't have control of your finances, you won't have peace. If you don't learn how to manage your money, your money will manage you. That increases your anxiety, and where there's anxiety, there is no peace.

This is how many Americans live. This might be how you live.

Jesus spoke about this. If you grew up in church, you've heard what he said. His words are rich and deep:

> "No one can serve two masters. Either you will hate the one and love the other, or you will be devoted to the one and despise the other. You cannot serve both God and money." Luke 16:13

You would expect Jesus to say you can't serve God and the devil or you can't serve God and sin. "You cannot serve both God and money" is unexpected. The Greek word that is translated "money" in the verse doesn't really mean "money." The word means all of your material possessions—*all your stuff.*

Jesus knew us well. He knew God's chief competitor for our devotion wouldn't be Satan. God's chief competitor for our devotion isn't even sin. God's chief competitors for our devotion are our stuff and our desire for more stuff. Our desire for money so we can have more stuff takes hold of our hearts.

To be devoted to something is to have our eyes on it. The object of our devotion becomes our primary decision-making filter. It drives the choices we make in life. It sets our priorities. When I begin to make decisions, I look through that filter of what I'm most devoted to. You may not bow down to money, but if you're like most people, when you measure your devotion to money against any other thing, you may have to conclude that you actually do love money.

"I WANT" IS BETTER THAN "I OWE"

Has your desire for money or stuff ever caused you to do something you regretted? Of course it has. We've all experienced that. You weren't the boss in that moment. Your devotion to your desire for getting what you wanted was the boss. It mastered you. Now, you're saddled with that lease payment, or you wish you'd bought a more affordable home, or you regret ever entering into that relationship. Now, you're filled with regret and discontentment.

Greed drives that discontentment. Most of us are greedy, but we have trouble seeing greed in the mirror. We assume only others are greedy. But we all struggle with greed as Jesus defined it. Greed is the assumption that everything we have is for our consumption. If we view everything that ends up in our hands as for us, we're greedy.

The problem is that greed is an appetite. Our desire for and devotion to acquire and consume are appetites. And like all appetites, they can never be fully and finally satisfied. We're tempted to spend everything that comes our way and then keep on spending once the money is gone. We're tempted to spend money we don't have to buy things we don't need. That's why our desire for stuff has the dangerous potential to crowd God out of our lives and become our master.

"I want" is always better than "I owe." It has the power to break the cycle of greed.

When you want something and don't have it, there's tension. When you owe on something and don't want to have to make payments on it, there's tension. We've all lived long enough to know which is the better tension. It's better to live with "I want and don't have" than "I owe and can't pay." You will be in one camp or another, because you'll always want stuff. But debt makes you a slave to your desires. And you can't be happy when you're a slave to debt.

"I want" is between you and God. It's an opportunity to pray to your heavenly Father: "God, I really want it." And then something relational happens. Maybe God says, "Not yet." Maybe he dings your conscience. Maybe he speaks to you through your spouse or a trusted friend. You know you can't have it because you can't afford it. That's disappointing, but you also know that chasing this thing you want will only lead to regret. It will only stand in God's place as the master of your life. No thing is worth that cost.

Again, the path of "I want" is relational. It's between you and God. But once you buy it, once you step on to the path of "I owe," it becomes an issue between you and a creditor. That dynamic tends to be a lot less relational, a lot less personal. And here's the worst part: God sides with the creditor, because if you're a Jesus follower, you have to pay your debts. And suddenly, the God who was trying to talk you out of "I owe" stands behind the creditor saying, "Pay up."

This is why Jesus said, "You cannot serve both God and money."

Watch the video segment for Session Three, using the space provided below to take notes on anything that stands out to you.

VIDEO NOTES

DISCUSSION QUESTIONS

1. Talk about a time when you thought a material possession would make you happy (we've all thought it). Did you acquire that possession? If so, how long did your happiness last?

2. Have you ever met someone who was happy despite having little money? If so, what stood out about that person?

3. Read Luke 16:10–13 below. What are some reasons it's so tempting for us to serve money instead of God?

    > Whoever can be trusted with very little can also be trusted with much, and whoever is dishonest with very little will also be dishonest with much. So if you have not been trustworthy in handling worldly wealth, who will trust you with true riches? And if you have not been trustworthy with someone else's property, who will give you property of your own? "No one can serve two masters. Either you will hate the one and love the other, or you will be devoted to the one and despise the other. You cannot serve both God and money." Luke 16:10–13

4. To what extent does discontentment currently drive your behavior and undermine your sense of peace?

5. During the message, Andy said, *"Giving will bring you joy, saving will you bring peace, and living on the rest will bring you freedom."* Is it difficult for you to believe that? Why or why not?

6. Is it more difficult for you to give, save, or live within your means? Why do you think that area of your finances is a struggle? What can you do this week to begin to reprioritize your finances? How can this group support you?

THINK ABOUT IT

No amount of money will eliminate your discontentment. No amount of money will eliminate your greed. How you manage the money you have is the only way to eliminate discontentment and greed. It's all about who or what is in control of your life. Is God in control or is your money in control?

No one can serve two masters.

Money won't make you happy, but money can contribute to your happiness if you manage it well. Generosity and wisdom with money will make you happy. Imagine if you'd been wise and generous with your money all along. You'd be happier. That's the direction in which Jesus leads those who will follow.

Wisdom and generosity look like this:

1. Give a percentage of your income to help others.
2. Save a percentage of your income.
3. Live on the rest.

BEFORE THE NEXT SESSION

Read pages 57–61 for an overview of next session's content.

SESSION FIVE

[**SHOES**]

In John 16:33, Jesus made a promise to his followers: "In this world you will have trouble." That promise is scary, but it's true. We all have trouble in life. We all hit bumps in the road. We all struggle from time to time. There's enough unavoidable pain in life without creating unnecessary pain for ourselves. Isn't that true?

Much of the time, trouble doesn't just come along. It's self-inflicted. We buy it, lease it, smoke it, drink it, or sleep with it. And then we're left to deal with the consequences and regret of our unwise decisions. You have more potential to steal from you, kill relationships, or destroy your life than anybody or anything else. You are your own worst enemy. You have done more to undermine your happiness than anyone else. You have the capacity to do more to undermine your happiness than anyone else.

You were there for every purchase, experience, poor decision, or sin that led to your unhappiness. You are the common denominator in every single event of your life. As much as we want to blame other people for our unhappiness, much of it is our own fault.

The good news is that Jesus spoke about the source of our unhappiness. He also gave us an alternative to help us avoid trouble:

> "The thief comes only to steal and kill and destroy; I have come that they may have life, and have it to the full. I am the good shepherd. The good shepherd lays down his life for the sheep." John 10:10–11

The "thief" Jesus mentions could be anything. Think about your life. Anyone or anything that gets between you and happiness is a thief. Anyone or anything that steals your potential, kills a relationship, or destroys your freedom is a thief. And, yes, the number one thief in your life is you.

What does it mean when Jesus calls himself the good shepherd? None of us likes to be compared to sheep, because sheep aren't bright enough to take care of themselves. But remember: most of our trouble is self-inflicted. Again, we bought it, leased it, smoked it, drank it, or slept with it. From Jesus' perspective, we have a lot in common with sheep. We hurt ourselves by chasing after all of the wrong things. That's why he offers himself as a good shepherd worth following. If someone is willing to lay down his life for you, he is *for* you. He is worth following.

In this session, we're going to explore two words: "happiness" and "pleasure." We'll take a look at the relationship between them.

PLEASURE BECOMES A PRISON

You may be your own worst enemy, but you're not your only enemy. Sin is your enemy too. Sin comes only to steal, kill, and destroy. We see that clearly in other people's lives but have a hard time seeing the damage sin does in our own lives.

Twenty-five or thirty years after Jesus' death and resurrection, the apostle Paul began writing letters to the churches he'd help plant along the Mediterranean rim. Those letters make up about two-thirds of what we know as the New Testament. In those letters, Paul contextualizes Jesus' teachings. In a letter he wrote to the church in Rome, Paul digs into our strange capacity to make ourselves unhappy and sin's role in those behaviors. What Paul uncovers is an important distinction. It's the difference between happiness and pleasure:

> Don't you know that when you offer yourselves to someone as obedient slaves, you are slaves of the one you obey—whether you are slaves to sin, which leads to death, or to obedience, which leads to righteousness?
>
> Romans 6:16

What Paul means is that if you repeatedly say yes to a pleasure, you will become its slave. At first, you choose that pleasure, but in time you lose control. If you choose something over and over, you eventually lose the ability to choose. The pleasure becomes a habit. It becomes a prison. At that point, you begin to feel the difference between pleasure and happiness. People in prison aren't happy. They aren't at peace with themselves, with other people, or with God.

Every time sin comes calling and you answer the door, you bring yourself closer to being its slave. And sin always leads to death. Sin always kills. It kills the way you view yourself. It kills your marriage. It kills your relationship with your kids. It kills your career. Wherever there is sin, something dies.

But Paul offers an alternative:

> But thanks be to God that, though you used to be slaves to sin, you have come to obey from your heart the pattern of teaching that has now claimed your allegiance. You have been set free from sin and have become slaves to righteousness. Romans 6:17–18

Either you offer yourself to sin, which leads to death, or you offer yourself to God through Christ, which leads to righteousness. By "righteousness" Paul means a right standing with God. He means that there is no relational tension between you and your heavenly Father. That leads to the full life Jesus promised because peace with God frees us to find peace with ourselves and equips us to make peace with others.

That is true happiness. It's superior in every way to the short-term pleasure sin offers us.

Watch the video segment for Session Three, using the space provided below to take notes on anything that stands out to you.

VIDEO NOTES

DISCUSSION QUESTIONS

1. Talk about something you do for fun. What do you enjoy about that hobby or activity?

2. Have you ever seen someone undermine his or her own happiness even though that person couldn't see it?

3. Think of a time when you ignored someone's good advice. What were some of the factors that caused you to ignore that wisdom?

4. Read John 10:7–11 below. What are some reasons it's difficult for people to believe that Jesus wants them to have life "to the full"?

> Therefore Jesus said again, "Very truly I tell you, I am the gate for the sheep. All who have come before me are thieves and robbers, but the sheep have not listened to them. I am the gate; whoever enters through me will be saved. They will come in and go out, and find pasture. The thief comes only to steal and kill and destroy; I have come that they may have life, and have it to the full. I am the good shepherd. The good shepherd lays down his life for the sheep." John 10:7–11

5. During the message, Andy said, *"Eventually, pleasure loses its pleasure and becomes a prison."* Is it difficult for you to believe that? Why or why not?

6. Is there a pleasure in your life that is stealing your freedom and undermining your happiness? If so, what is one thing you can do this week to begin to trade your sin for the good shepherd? How can this group support you?

THINK ABOUT IT

Is there a pleasure that is undermining your happiness? Is there a pleasure that's beginning to act like a warden in your life by taking away your freedom to say no? If so, you've prioritized your pleasure over your happiness. The moment you quit prioritizing your pleasure over your happiness, it will be a good day for you and for everyone who loves you and depends on you. Maybe it's time to trade your sin for a good shepherd who offers you life to the full.

BEFORE THE NEXT SESSION

Read pages 67–73 for an overview of next session's content.

SESSION SIX

[YOU'RE NOT ENOUGH]

What makes you happy?

No *thing*. We said in Session One that no thing makes us happy. Happiness always includes a who or two. We can't be happy without healthy relationships. We were designed to live in community.

What makes you happy?

Sowing. Jesus said that happiness is not immediately accessible. It can't be found or bought. It's an outcome. You sow your way into happiness. You make decisions that eventually reap happiness. Many of those decisions—like not buying that new car we can't afford—cost us pleasure in the short-term but pay off with happiness in the long-term. This idea is so counterintuitive in our culture that if you haven't experienced it, you may not believe it.

During this final session, we're going to explore one final truth about happiness. It has to do with you. Here it is:

You can't fulfill you.

You need more than you have to offer. If you were able to be everything you've always wanted to be and have everything you've always wanted to have, you wouldn't be happy. It wouldn't be enough. You cannot find happiness by working as hard as you can to create the ideal version of yourself. If you want to be happy, you have to turn your vision outward.

Researchers at the University of Chicago asked the question, "What are the most fulfilling careers?" They collected a list of responses and then sorted those responses into categories. They found that people are most fulfilled in their work when they:

- Care for others
- Teach others
- Protect others
- Pursue creativity

The researchers discovered no correlation between income and job satisfaction or happiness once a person reached the point where he or she could afford to eat and pay the bills.

Another group of researchers in Britain asked the question, "Is there a correlation between happiness and selflessness?" They reviewed 40 studies that had been conducted over a period of 20 years. They found a link between three ideas:

1. Volunteering
2. Health
3. Happiness

If you make a lifestyle of volunteering in your community or your church, your chances of suffering depression, heart disease, and stress go way down. Teenagers who systematically volunteer somewhere have lower incidences of drug use and unplanned pregnancies. That's true even if a teenager is forced to serve by his or her parents.

Our natural inclination is to acquire and to consume. Our natural inclination is to pay attention to ourselves. How is it that behaving selflessly makes us happier? Why does emptying ourselves leave us feeling so full?

DIVINE DESIGN

It's no mistake that selflessness makes us happy. This is by divine design. We were made to be selfless. God created us to live with open hands. Selfishness is the result of our brokenness.

Sin has a tendency to isolate each of us into his or her own self-centered world. Sin isolates us from one another. Sin tells us to spend our time and money on ourselves. Sin says that if we fill ourselves up, we'll be happy. Yet observation, experience, and even investigation say the opposite. We are most filled up when we pour ourselves out.

If that seems counterintuitive, look no further than the happiest people you know. Aren't they the most selfless people you know? You wouldn't necessarily want to look like them. You wouldn't want to make as little money as they do. You wouldn't want to drive the same kind of car they drive. But they live with a peace you envy.

You strive. You're discontent. They seem calm and at ease. Happy people find a way to give their lives away.

The apostle Paul wrote a letter to Christians in the Roman province of Galatia. We call it the book of Galatians. In that letter, Paul makes an observation about two different approaches to living:

> The acts of the flesh are obvious: sexual immorality, impurity and debauchery; idolatry and witchcraft; hatred, discord, jealousy, fits of rage, selfish ambition, dissensions, factions and envy; drunkenness, orgies, and the like. I warn you, as I did before, that those who live like this will not inherit the kingdom of God.

> But the fruit of the Spirit is love, joy, peace, forbearance, kindness, goodness, faithfulness, gentleness and self-control. Against such things there is no law.
>
> Galatians 5:19–23

This passage captures the stark contrast between living for yourself and pouring yourself out and finding happiness. Last session, we explored the difference between pleasure and happiness. We said that if you prioritize pleasure, you'll become a slave to sin. But if you prioritize happiness, you'll be free.

When Paul talks about "the acts of the flesh," he means your behavior if you were to do whatever you wanted to do. He means the way you'd behave if there were no consequences. These are your natural impulses. Idolatry is trying to manipulate God into doing your bidding. Witchcraft is trying to harness the forces of nature to do your bidding. We know what hatred, discord, jealousy, fits of rage, selfish ambition, dissensions, factions and envy, drunkenness, orgies, and the like are. They are pleasures at someone else's expense. When we give into our selfishness, our pleasures always cost someone else. That cost may be relational, emotional, or spiritual.

The desires of the flesh are appetites. And appetites are never fully and finally satisfied. When you feed an appetite, it grows. When you can't satisfy an appetite, you become frustrated and angry. If you say yes to the sinful desires in order to try to fill yourself up, it will leave you wanting more.

The opposite of the desires of the flesh is the fruit of the Spirit. Living by the fruit of the Spirit means surrendering to God. It means not trying to satisfy our natural appetites. Paul says that we were made to live by the fruit of the Spirit. We flourish in that kind of life. Imagine living in a family characterized by love, joy, peace, patience, kindness, goodness, faithfulness, gentleness, and self-control. Would you be happy? Of course you would.

You were designed to exist in a community of people living out the fruit of the Spirit. It is an others-focused way of life. Paul writes of that kind of life: "Against such things there is no law." The fruit of the Spirit are self-regulating and others-focused. They don't require judges, juries, or police officers to make sure everyone is being treated fairly. No one is taken advantage of when people live by the fruit of the Spirit. No one loses.

Life by the Spirit is free. It is life to the full. It is what makes you happy.

Watch the video segment for Session Three, using the space provided below to take notes on anything that stands out to you.

VIDEO NOTES

DISCUSSION QUESTIONS

1. Talk about a time when acting selflessly made you happier. Why do you think you felt happy?

2. It's easy for us to agree that we can't find happiness through money, possessions, and status. Why is it so difficult for us to live as though that's true?

3. During the message, Andy said, *"You were designed to live with open hands. Selfishness is the result of brokenness."* Is this difficult for you to believe? Why or why not?

4. Read Galatians 5:19–21 below. In what ways are you tempted to find happiness at the expense of others? How do you avoid acting on those temptations?

> The acts of the flesh are obvious: sexual immorality, impurity and debauchery; idolatry and witchcraft; hatred, discord, jealousy, fits of rage, selfish ambition, dissensions, factions and envy; drunkenness, orgies, and the like. I warn you, as I did before, that those who live like this will not inherit the kingdom of God. Galatians 5:19–21

5. Read Galatians 5:22–23 below. As you look at this list of behaviors, is it difficult for you to believe they lead to happiness? Why or why not?

> But the fruit of the Spirit is love, joy, peace, forbearance, kindness, goodness, faithfulness, gentleness and self-control. Against such things there is no law. Galatians 5:22–23

6. Is there a way you need to serve others or a place you need to volunteer? If so, what is one step you can take this week toward serving or volunteering? How can this group support you?

THINK ABOUT IT

You were made for more than you. It's not intuitive, but it's true. You can't acquire or consume your way to happiness. But you may be able to serve and volunteer your way there. If you live as if it's all about you, you will never be happy.

The value of a life is measured by how much of it was given away. That's what we celebrate in the lives of others. We intuitively know that it's what's most valuable. When a person lives a selfless life, we see greatness. We know that person has lived well, that his or her life has meaning. People like that have discovered the secret to happiness: *pouring out is what fills us up*. If you want to be happy, you have to find a way to give your life away.

[LEADER'S GUIDE]

This *Leader's Guide* is available in PDF format on

GroupLeaders.org/WhatMakesYouHappy.

LEADING THE DISCUSSION

If you find yourself as the lead facilitator of the Discussion Questions, here are three things to consider during your group meetings:

CULTIVATE DISCUSSION

It is the ideas of everyone in the group that make a group meeting successful. Your role as the facilitator is to create an environment in which people feel safe to share their thoughts.

STAY ON TRACK

While you want to leave space for group members to think through the discussion, make sure the conversation is contributing to the topic being discussed that session.

Don't let it veer off on tangents. Go with the flow, but be ready to nudge the conversation in the right direction when necessary.

PRAY

This is the most important thing you can do as a group. Pray that God is not only present at your group meetings, but that he is directing them.

[A TYPICAL GROUP MEETING]

Social Time	30 minutes
Video	20 minutes
Discussion	55 minutes
Prayer	15 minutes

SESSION ONE
NOTES FOR LEADING

BIG IDEA

No thing can make you happy. Happy is about who, not what.

To prepare to lead the first session:

- Read Matthew 22:34–40, and use the Reflect and Pray sections below to consider the verses you've read.
- Read the session materials, watch the video, and look through the Discussion Questions.

REFLECT

Sin separates us from others. Sin separates us from God. Sin separates us from ourselves. When we sin, we replace happiness with pleasure, people with things, intimacy with images, exclusivity with experience, the ultimate for the immediate, self-control for self-expression. Sin promises us happiness but can't keep that promise.

Sin is not your friend.

Peace with God paves the way for peace with yourself and equips you to make peace with others. Since Jesus valued and prioritized peace with God, others, and us, and since you want to be happy, follow Jesus.

In what are you currently seeking happiness? What are some practical things you can do today and for the rest of the week to turn your attention to Jesus as your source of happiness?

PRAY

Spend a few moments praying that God will help you identify the things you look to for happiness. Be humble. Ask him to forgive your sins. Know that he loves you and never withholds forgiveness.

Now spend a few moments quietly listening to God. You probably won't hear an audible voice, but the Holy Spirit might convict you, making you more aware of how you look for happiness in things instead of relationships.

DISCUSSION QUESTIONS

1. What is the first thing that comes to mind when you think about what makes you happy? Why do you think that comes to mind?

2. How would you define the word "happiness"? How do you think your definition has influenced the ways you've chosen to pursue happiness?

    The first two questions are opportunities to take the pulse of your group members. Since our definitions drive our assumptions, it's helpful to know how your group members define happiness and how they pursue it in their lives.

3. Read Matthew 22:35–40. Respond to Jesus' statement. Does it sound too easy? Why or why not?

4. During the message, Andy said that sin separates us from ourselves, others, and God by enticing us to substitute things for relationships. Do you believe this to be true? Why or why not?

    Questions 3 and 4 initiate a redefinition. As you and your group members discuss the passage from Matthew as well as the video message, you'll begin to explore the idea of happiness grounded in healthy relationships instead of things like money and success.

WHAT MAKES YOU HAPPY

5. Are you at peace with yourself, others, and God? If not, what's getting in the way of your peace in those relationships?

6. In *what* are you currently seeking happiness? What is one thing you can do this week to turn your attention to Jesus as your source of happiness? What can this group do to support you?

   Questions 5 and 6 challenge you and your group members to personalize this new definition and begin to apply it in your own lives. How are you off course? How are you seeking happiness in the wrong places? How can you get back on course?

   Remember: This is just the beginning of the conversation. In the sessions to come, you'll dig more deeply into how to change the way you seek happiness.

SESSION TWO
NOTES FOR LEADING

BIG IDEA

Happiness is not immediately accessible. It is a result governed by the principle of sowing and reaping.

To prepare to lead the second session:

- Read Matthew 5:3–10, and use the Reflect and Pray sections below to consider the verses you've read.

- Read the session materials, watch the video, and look through the Discussion Questions.

REFLECT

Happy people embrace their daily dependence on God regardless of what they have or the circumstances they face. They don't hide from the bad, unjust, and random aspects of life. They aren't afraid to hurt. They embrace the reality that they are not the center of the universe. Happy people focus on God's glory and the welfare of others.

Trying to be the center of the universe is exhausting. Trying to control the outcomes of your circumstances is impossible. The moment you put your trust in riches, instead of him who richly provides, you will be unhappy. We find happiness when we accept and declare that we are dependent on God.

What do you need to "sow" in your life right now so that you can "reap" happiness in the future?

PRAY

Begin your day by declaring your dependence on your heavenly Father for provision, pardon, and protection. Thank him for his mercy, grace, faithfulness, and love. Ask him to help you see others the way he sees them and to treat them accordingly.

DISCUSSION QUESTIONS

1. Last week, you were challenged to turn your attention to Jesus as your source of happiness. How did it go?

   Question one is a simple icebreaker that helps you reflect on your previous discussion. Be prepared to share your own experiences.

2. How would you define the word "holiness"? How do you think your definition has influenced your relationship with God?

   As we noted last week, definitions matter. How your group members define holiness may tell you about how they view and relate to God. Do they define it relationally or in terms of religious duty? Since "holiness" isn't a word we use in everyday conversations, this question may be met with silence. That's okay. Try to be comfortable in the silence. Try to give your group members time to think before offering your own definition.

3. Read Matthew 5:3–12. Do you have trouble believing that happiness follows from the list of behaviors Jesus describes? Why or why not?

   This question gives group members who have trouble believing or understanding the passage of Scripture an opportunity to voice their objections or ask questions. Don't shut down discussion by offering simple answers. Often, those answers communicate that the group isn't a safe place for open discussion rather than actually addressing a group member's objections or questions. Instead, thank the person for being willing to share, acknowledge that Scripture is often counterintuitive, and ask clarifying questions (e.g., "Who do you think Jesus had in mind when he talked about 'the meek'?"). This approach helps group members think for themselves.

4. What are some reasons it's difficult for us to live as though we're dependent on God? What do we lose when we live like that? What do we gain?

   Treat this question like a brainstorming session. Lots of ideas are better than a few. No idea is a bad idea.

5. Read Matthew 7:24–26. To what extent have you built your life upon dependence on God? How do you think that has affected your happiness?

6. If happiness is powered by the law of the harvest, what do you need to "sow" in your life right now so that you can "reap" happiness in the future? How can this group support you?

   Questions 5 and 6 challenge you and your group members to think about the big idea in the context of your own lives and begin to apply what you've learned. Challenge your group members (and yourself) to be concrete and specific when it comes to changing what you're sowing in your lives right now. Commit to encouraging one another and holding one another accountable.

SESSION THREE
NOTES FOR LEADING

BIG IDEA

Peace with God is possible because God has made peace with you.

To prepare to lead the third session:

- Read 1 John 4:7–21, and use the Reflect and Pray sections below to consider the verses you've read.
- Read the session materials, watch the video, and look through the Discussion Questions.

REFLECT

Peace with God is only possible because God has already made peace with you through Jesus. You can experience that peace when you stop resisting and decide to surrender to your heavenly Father. That's easy to understand but difficult to do. It's an ongoing effort, carried out over a lifetime.

What stands in the way of your peace with God? What is one thing you can do this week to surrender that area of your life to your heavenly Father?

PRAY

Read verses 16–19 aloud as a prayer, replacing "we" and "us" with "I" and "me," and "God" and "he" with "you." Ask your heavenly Father to give you the strength and courage to love others fearlessly.

DISCUSSION QUESTIONS

1. Do you agree that peace with God paves the way to peace with ourselves and equips us to make peace with others? Why or why not?

2. To what extent do you think the word "sin" is relevant to your relationship with God?

   This question should begin by defining the word "sin." Because "sin" isn't a word we typically use outside of its religious context, it may take some time and thought for your group members to come up with a working definition. It's less important that their definitions be theologically precise than that they give you a sense of how they think sin influences their relationship with God (e.g., do they believe God's grace is at the center of that relationship or are they trying to earn his love and acceptance?).

3. Read Romans 5:1–2. Does peace with God through Jesus Christ sound too easy? Why or why not?

   Encourage your group to push past the easy "church" answer to this question. Even when we know that God is merciful and full of grace, why is it so difficult for us not to try to earn our way to peace with him?

4. Read 1 John 4:20. What does this verse say about how God values you and other people? In what ways does it challenge your assumptions about what it means to have a relationship with God?

   What John wrote in this verse is radical: our vertical relationship with God is reflected in our horizontal relationships with people (whom he created in his image). If we don't love people, we don't love God. Don't shy away from talking about the tensions this creates in our hearts and lives.

5. Talk about a time when you were in conflict with someone. How did that conflict affect your relationship with God?

6. What stands in the way of your peace with God? What's one thing you can do this week to begin to surrender that area of your life? What can this group do to support you?

   Questions 5 and 6 challenge you and your group members to think about the big idea in the context of your own lives and begin to apply what you've learned. This session's application question is especially challenging because it may involve removing things you enjoy (but that are getting in the way of peace with God) from your lives. Challenge your group mem-

bers (and yourself) to be concrete and specific about what you'll do. Commit to encouraging one another and holding one another accountable.

SESSION FOUR
NOTES FOR LEADING

BIG IDEA

Money won't make you happy, but it will contribute to your happiness if you manage it well.

To prepare to lead the fourth session:

- Read Luke 16:1–13, and use the Reflect and Pray sections that below to consider the verses you've read.
- Read the session materials, watch the video, and look through the Discussion Questions.

REFLECT

Money won't make you happy, but money can contribute to your happiness if you manage it well. Be generous. Be wise. Give to those in need. Save for the future. Live within your means. When you are a good steward of your finances, you will find peace.

Do you need to do a better job of giving, saving, or living within your means? Consider your first step to being a better financial steward. If necessary, seek wise counsel.

PRAY

Take a few minutes to speak with your heavenly Father. Thank him for all he has given. Ask him to give you the wisdom and courage to be a wise and generous steward.

DISCUSSION QUESTIONS

1. Talk about a time when you thought a material possession would make you happy (we've all thought it). Did you acquire that possession? If so, how long did your happiness last?

    This question is an icebreaker. The discussion doesn't need to be heavy or theologically deep. We've all made the mistake of thinking a "thing" could make us happy. In retrospect, that assumption can seem silly (and humorous).

2. Have you ever met someone who was happy despite having little money? If so, what stood out about that person?

    Don't fish for specific answers or insights. Spend more time listening than offering opinions. See where your group members take the conversation. In this stage of the discussion, it's

okay if "What stood out about that person?" doesn't lead to
talk about faith or God.

3. Read Luke 16:10–13. What are some reasons it's so tempting for us to serve money instead of God?

4. To what extent does discontentment currently drive your
   behavior and undermine your sense of peace?

   Questions 3 and 4 allow you and your group members to
   reflect on our culture's priorities and how those priorities
   influence your assumptions about how life and the world
   operate.

5. During the message, Andy said, *"Giving will bring you joy,*
   saving will bring you peace, and living on the rest will bring
   you freedom." Is it difficult for you to believe that? Why or
   why not?

   This question gives group members who disagree with
   Andy's central premise the opportunity to voice their objec-
   tions or ask questions. Don't shut down discussion by rebut-
   ting or offering simple answers. Instead, thank the person for
   being willing to share. Ask clarifying questions (e.g., "What
   are the risks of making giving and saving your top financial
   priorities?"). This approach helps group members think for
   themselves.

6. Is it more difficult for you to give, save, or live within your
   means? Why do you think that area of your finances is a
   struggle? What can you do this week to begin to reprioritize
   your finances? How can this group support you?

The questions in number 6 challenge you and your group members to think about the big idea in the context of your own lives and begin to apply what you've learned. Shifting your financial priorities is too big a task to happen in a single group meeting or even a single week. The goal for you and your group members should be to take a next step. Depending on the current state of your finances, that next step may be giving a percentage of your income. It may be creating a budget so you know where your money is going. It may be meeting with a financial professional to determine how you can get out of debt. Challenge your group members (and yourself) to be concrete and specific about what they'll do. Commit to encouraging one another and holding one another accountable.

SESSION FIVE
NOTES FOR LEADING

BIG IDEA

Prioritize happiness over pleasure and you'll have both. If you reverse it, sin will be your master and you'll have neither.

To prepare to lead the fifth session:

- Read John 10:1–16, and use the Reflect and Pray sections below to consider the verses you've read.

- Read the session materials, watch the video, and look through the Discussion Questions.

REFLECT

Read the passage aloud. As you read it, think about what it says about how sheep depend on their shepherds for comfort, protection, and the basic necessities of life. What would your life look like if you depended on Jesus like sheep depend on their shepherds? How would it influence your decision making? How would it change your heart?

Is sin stealing your freedom and undermining your happiness? What is one thing you can do to surrender your life—and that sin—to your Good Shepherd?

PRAY

Thank God for all he provides in your life. Acknowledge that all you have comes from him. Ask him to help you remember your dependence and to find happiness through that dependence.

DISCUSSION QUESTIONS

1. Talk about something you do for fun. What do you enjoy about that hobby or activity?

   This is a simple icebreaker. Keep the discussion light, fun, and relational. This is an opportunity to learn something new about your group members.

2. Have you ever seen someone undermine his or her own happiness and that person couldn't see it?

This question is designed to help you and your group members begin to wrestle with the tension between happiness and pleasure. Because it's based on your observations of other people, it's a safe question that pushes you in the direction of deeper discussion.

3. Think of a time when you ignored someone's good advice. What were some of the factors that caused you to ignore that wisdom?

4. Read John 10:7–11. What are some reasons it's difficult for people to believe that Jesus wants them to have life "to the full"?

    Questions 3 and 4 challenge you and your group members to think about how your desires for short-term pleasure influence the ways you think about and apply the wisdom you receive from others . . . including the wisdom you receive from Jesus.

5. During the message, Andy said, *"Eventually, pleasure loses its pleasure and becomes a prison."* Is it difficult for you to believe that? Why or why not?

    This questions gives group members who disagree with Andy's central premise the opportunity to voice their objections or ask questions. Don't shut down discussion by rebutting or offering simple answers. Instead, thank the person for being willing to share. Ask clarifying questions (e.g., "Can you think of a time in your own life when a pleasure didn't lose its pleasure and become a prison?"). This approach helps group members think for themselves.

6. Is there a pleasure in your life that is stealing your freedom and undermining your happiness? If so, what is one thing you can do this week to begin to trade your sin for the good shepherd? How can this group support you?

These questions challenge you and your group members to think about the big idea in the context of your own lives and begin to apply what you've learned. As with Session 3, these application questions are especially challenging because it may involve removing things you enjoy from your lives. Challenge your group members (and yourself) to be concrete and specific about what they'll do. Commit to encouraging one another and holding one another accountable.

SESSION SIX

NOTES FOR LEADING

BIG IDEA

You can't acquire, consume, or exercise your way to happiness. But you may be able to serve and volunteer your way there.

To prepare to lead the sixth session:

- Read Galatians 5:13–26, and use the Reflect and Pray sections below to consider the verses you've read.
- Read the session materials, watch the video, and look through the Discussion Questions.

REFLECT

As you were reading, did any of the words in verses 19 through 23 stand out to you? If so, write them down. Think about why those words are significant for you. Do they represent values you hold dear? Are they indicators of opportunities for growth?

Remember: selfishness is natural, but you were not designed for selfishness.

Is there an opportunity for serving others or volunteering somewhere that you're missing out on? If so, what is one step you can take immediately to take advantage of that opportunity?

PRAY

Spend a few moments quietly listening to God, knowing that he wants you to rest in him. Thank your heavenly Father for making you in his image. Ask him to identify your own tendencies toward selfishness and to help you rise above them by giving him control and giving yourself to others.

DISCUSSION QUESTIONS

1. Talk about a time when acting selflessly made you happier. Why do you think you felt happy?

   This question is an icebreaker. The discussion doesn't need to be heavy or theologically deep. Listen closely to your group members' reasons why selflessness has made them happy in the past. It may shape the direction of the conversation to come.

2. It's easy for us to agree that we can't find happiness through money, possessions, and status. Why is it so difficult to live as though that's true?

   This question pokes at our cultural assumptions. When our cultural priorities conflict with the priorities of Scripture, why is it so difficult to see past culture even when we trust and believe the Bible?

3. During the message, Andy said, *"You were designed to live with open hands. Selfishness is the result of brokenness."* Is this difficult for you to believe? Why or why not?

   This question gives group members who disagree with Andy's central premise the opportunity to voice their objections or ask questions. Listen. Don't shut down discussion by rebutting or offering simple answers. Thank the person for being willing to share. Ask clarifying questions (e.g., "What are the risks of selflessness? Do you think there are any rewards associated with it?"). This approach helps group members think for themselves.

4. Read Galatians 5:19–21. In what ways are you tempted to find happiness at the expense of others? How do you avoid acting on those temptations?

5. Read Galatians 5:22–23. As you look at this list of behaviors, is it difficult for you to believe they lead to happiness? Why or why not?

   Questions 4 and 5 are designed to encourage an extended conversation about this session's key passage of Scripture and how it applies to your lives. Question 4 focuses on the acts of the flesh (pleasure), while Question 5 focuses on the fruit of the Spirit (happiness). As the group's leader, you can influence how much others are willing to share. Be ready to lead the conversation by being transparent about your own struggles and victories.

6. Is there a way you need to serve others or a place you need to volunteer? If so, what is one step you can take this week toward serving or volunteering? How can this group support you?

These questions challenge you and your group members to think about the big idea in the context of your own lives and begin to apply what you've learned. They offer opportunities for personal as well as group application. Each member should consider how he or she can serve others. You might also consider how you can serve together as a group. Commit to encouraging one another and holding one another accountable.

NOTES

NOTES

NOTES

NOTES

Why in the World DVD Study

The Reason God Became One of Us

Andy Stanley

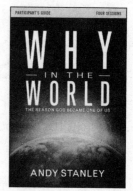

In this four-session video Bible study, best-selling author and pastor Andy Stanley takes a closer look at one of the unique things Christians believe: God became one of us. Why in the world would God do that?

Why would God leave the comfort and recognition of heaven to live on this ball of dirt in a time before morphine and indoor plumbing, when the best of conditions barely paralleled the worst of modern-day conditions? Why?

We think we know why he died. But what compelled him to live as one of us?

Session Titles

1. To Communicate and Demonstrate
2. Like Son, Like Father
3. Classless
4. Putting Religion in Its Place

Available in stores and online!

The New Rules for Love, Sex, and Dating DVD Study

Are you the person you are looking for is looking for?

Andy Stanley

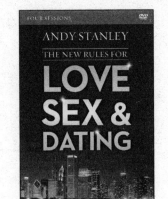

Single? Looking for the "right person"? Thinking that if you met the "right person" everything would turn out "right"? Think again. In this video-based small group Bible study, Andy Stanley explores the challenges, assumptions, and land mines associated with dating in the twenty-first century. Best of all, he offers the most practical and uncensored advice you will ever hear on this topic.

Not for the faint of heart, *The New Rules for Love, Sex, and Dating DVD Study* challenges singles to step up and set a new standard for this generation.

> *"If you don't want a marriage like the majority of marriages, then stop dating like the majority of daters!"*
>
> — Andy Stanley

Session Titles

1. The Right Person Myth
2. The Gentleman's Club
3. Designer Sex
4. If I Were You

Available in stores and online!

Starting Point DVD and Conversation Guide, Revised Edition

A Conversation about Faith

Andy Stanley and the Starting Point Team

Everything has a starting point—your life, your relationships, your education, your career.

Sometimes we forget that faith has a starting point as well. For some of us, our faith journeys began in childhood as a set of beliefs handed to us by a parent, teacher, or pastor. Maybe you developed a framework of faith based on personal experience. Or maybe you had no faith at all. Too often, a faith formed in childhood isn't strong enough to withstand the pressures of adult life.

But what if you could find a new starting point for faith?

Welcome to Starting Point—an 8-session small group conversation about faith. Whether you're new to faith, curious about God, or coming back to church after some time away, it's a place where your opinions and beliefs are valued, and no question is off limits.

During the eight sessions, you will:
- Use the *Starting Point Conversation Guide* to reflect on central questions of faith and life.
- Watch the video component each week in preparation or as part of the discussion.
- Explore and share what you're learning with other people in a conversational environment.

Come as you are and build relationships with others as you discover your starting point.

Available in stores and online!

Follow DVD Study

No Experience Necessary

Andy Stanley

Lots of people think Christianity is all about doing what Jesus says. But what if doing what Jesus says isn't what Jesus says to do at all? Jesus' invitation is an invitation to relationship, and it begins with a simple request: follow me.

Religion says "Change and you can join us." Jesus says, "Join us and you will change." There's a huge difference. Jesus doesn't expect people to be perfect. He just wants them to follow him. Being a sinner doesn't disqualify anyone. Being an unbeliever doesn't disqualify anyone. In fact, following almost always begins with a sinner and unbeliever taking one small step.

In this eight-session video-based Bible study (participant's guide sold separately), Andy Stanley takes small groups on a journey through the Gospels as he traces Jesus' teaching on what it means to follow.

Sessions include:

1. Jesus Says
2. Next Steps
3. Fearless
4. Follow Wear
5. The Fine Print
6. What I Want to Want
7. Leading Great
8. Unfollow

Available in stores and online!